Diwali
Story Book for Kids

Ambsachi Nila

All rights reserved.
No part of this publication may be reproduced, disseminated or transmitted in any form or by any means, including photocopying, recording or other electronic methods
without the prior written permission of the publisher,
except for brief quotations in critical reviews
and certain other non-commercial uses permitted by copyright law.

Diwali

(Dipawali) is a Hindu Festival of Light.

Diwali is a movable holiday, usually falling in mid-autumn, in late October or early November.

It is celebrated every year in India for 5 days.

The date of Diwali is determined by the Hindu calendar, according to which the month begins just after the full moon

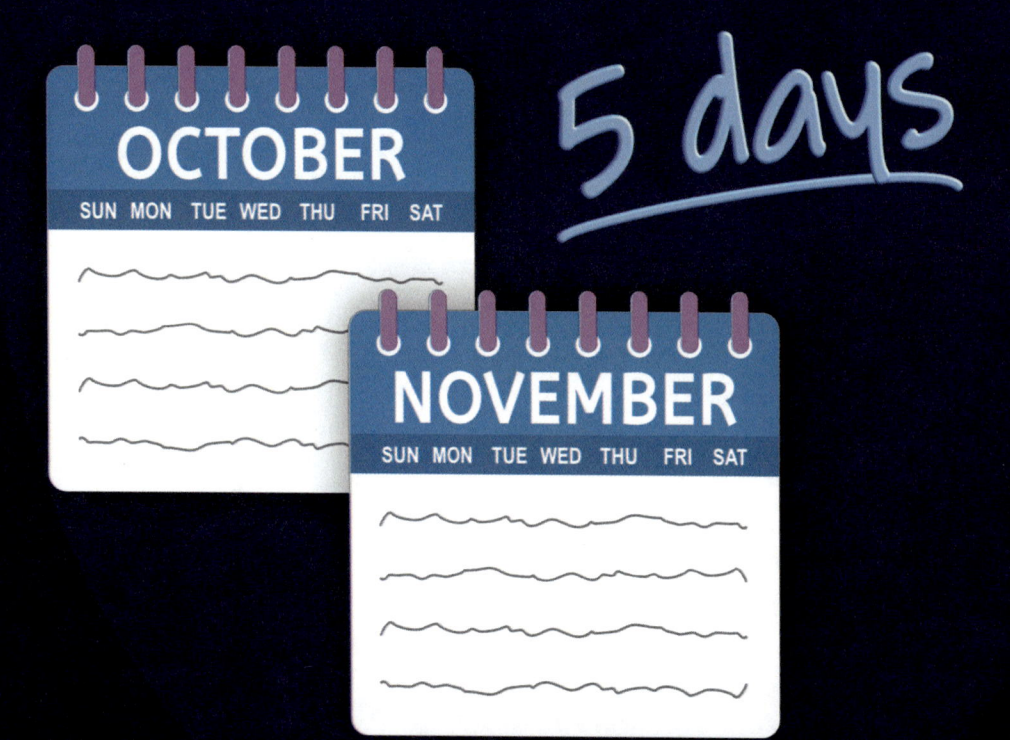

Rashi	#	Month
Mina	1	Mar
Mesha	2	Apr
Vrisha	3	May
Mithuna	4	Jun
Karka	5	Jul
Singa	6	Aug
Kanya	7	Sep
Tula	8	Oct
Vrischika	9	Nov
Dhanus	10	Dec
Makara	11	Jan
Kumbha	12	Feb

Diwali →

The word **Dipawali** literally means "**row of lamps**." It was formed by combining the words **dipa** ("lamp") and **awali** ("row"). The word refers to olive lamps fired from clay, which are lit in front of every house during Diwali.

The lamps symbolize the victory of light over darkness - good over evil.

This is the main theme of the entire Diwali celebration.

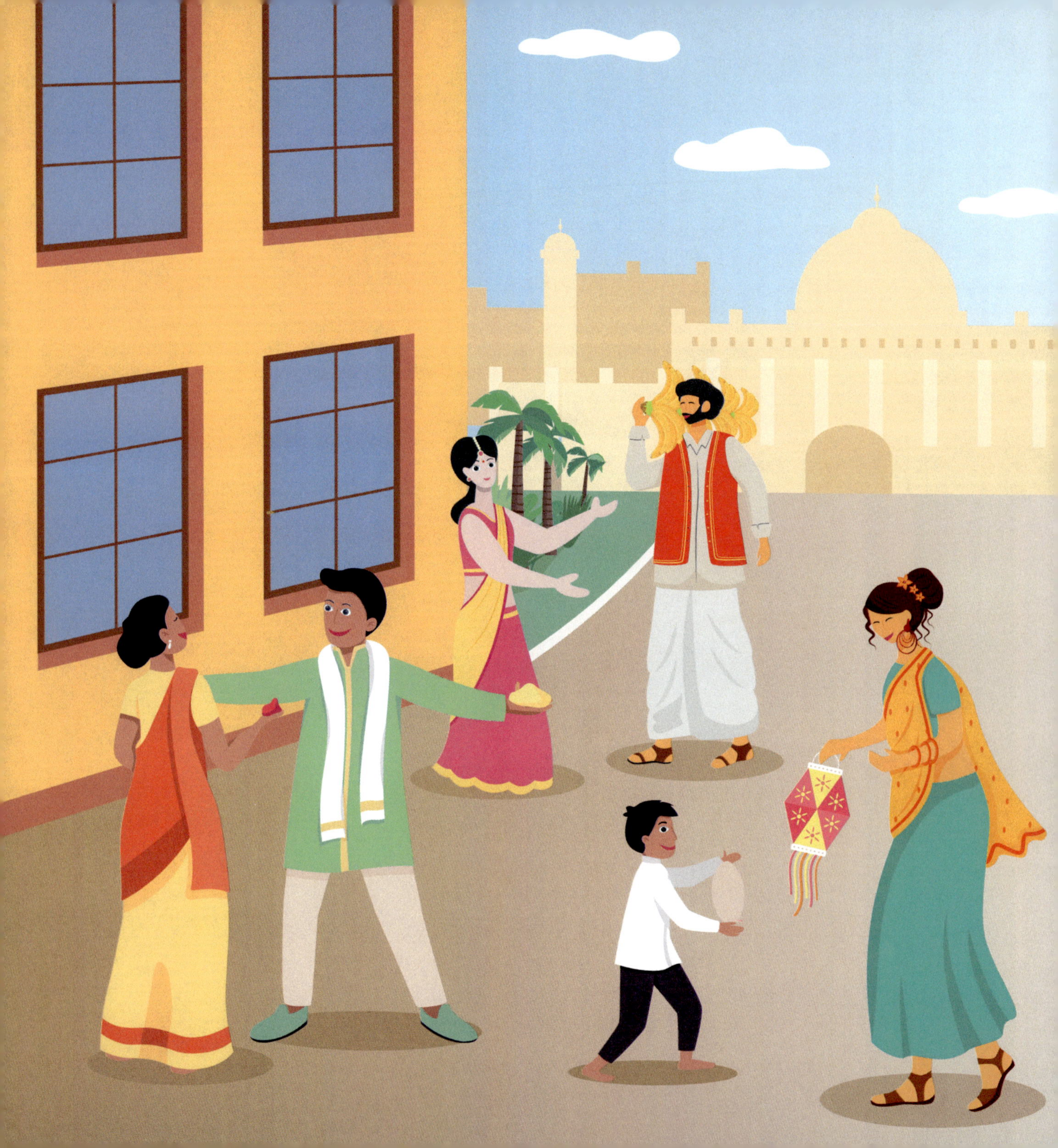

Diwali is one of the most important traditional and joyous holidays celebrated in India. Every year it is celebrated on a grand scale. During the celebration there are numerous cultural events, prayers, dances or preparing and eating meals together. Everyone spends this period with family and friends. It is very common for loved ones to give each other gifts and sweets. The setting of the festival is enhanced by fireworks and floral decorations. Diwali is also a time of great shopping for Indians.

HISTORY

The celebration of Diwali refers to the battle between **Prince Rama** and the demon **Ravana**, described in the epic **"Ramayana"**. The demon abducted the prince's beloved wife **Sita** and imprisoned her on the island of Ceylon.

Sita

Ravana →

Sita is considered one of the incarnations of Lakshmi, the goddess of happiness, prosperity and abundance. Prince Rama won his battle with the demon, and his loyal people, wishing to celebrate the couple's return home and their victory over the evil personified by the demon, lit their way with rows of olive lamps.

During the Festival of Light, followers of Hinduism commemorate the victorious battle of good over evil by setting up hundreds of lights in the streets.

Each of the five days of Diwali celebrations has a distinct meaning and its own name.

DIYA

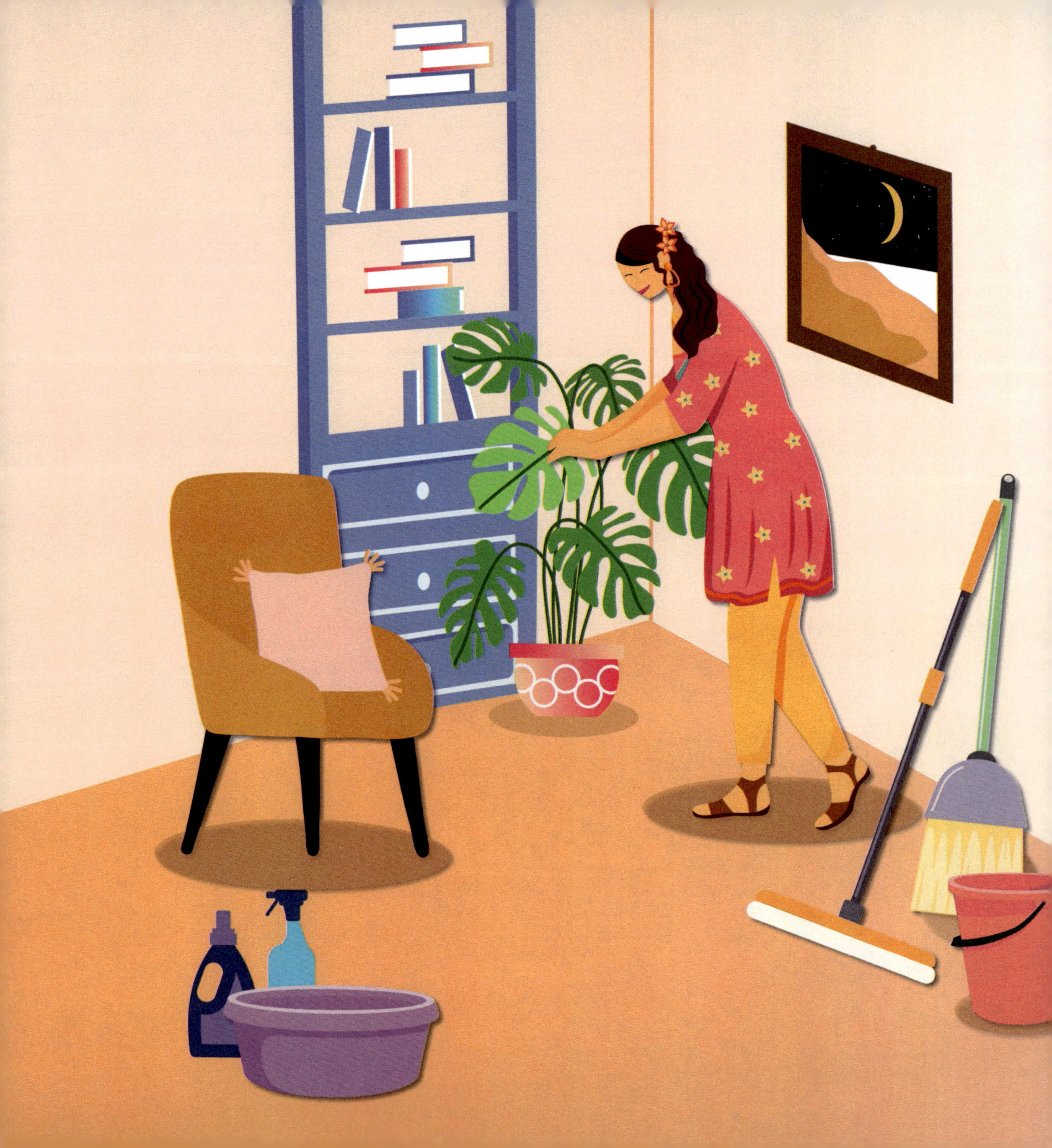

DAY 1
Dhanteras

It is a day of cleaning and preparing one's homes for the coming of the gods. On this day, some people take a ritual bath to wash away the dirt of the entire previous year. On the first day of Diwali, Indians often buy gifts for their loved ones.

RANGOLI

DAY 2
Naraka Chaturdasi

This is the day when houses are decorated with lights and **rangoli** are laid out on the floors.

Perishable materials such as colored powders and sand are used to symbolize the impermanence of the world.

On this day, desserts and sweets are prepared, which are an integral part of the festival.

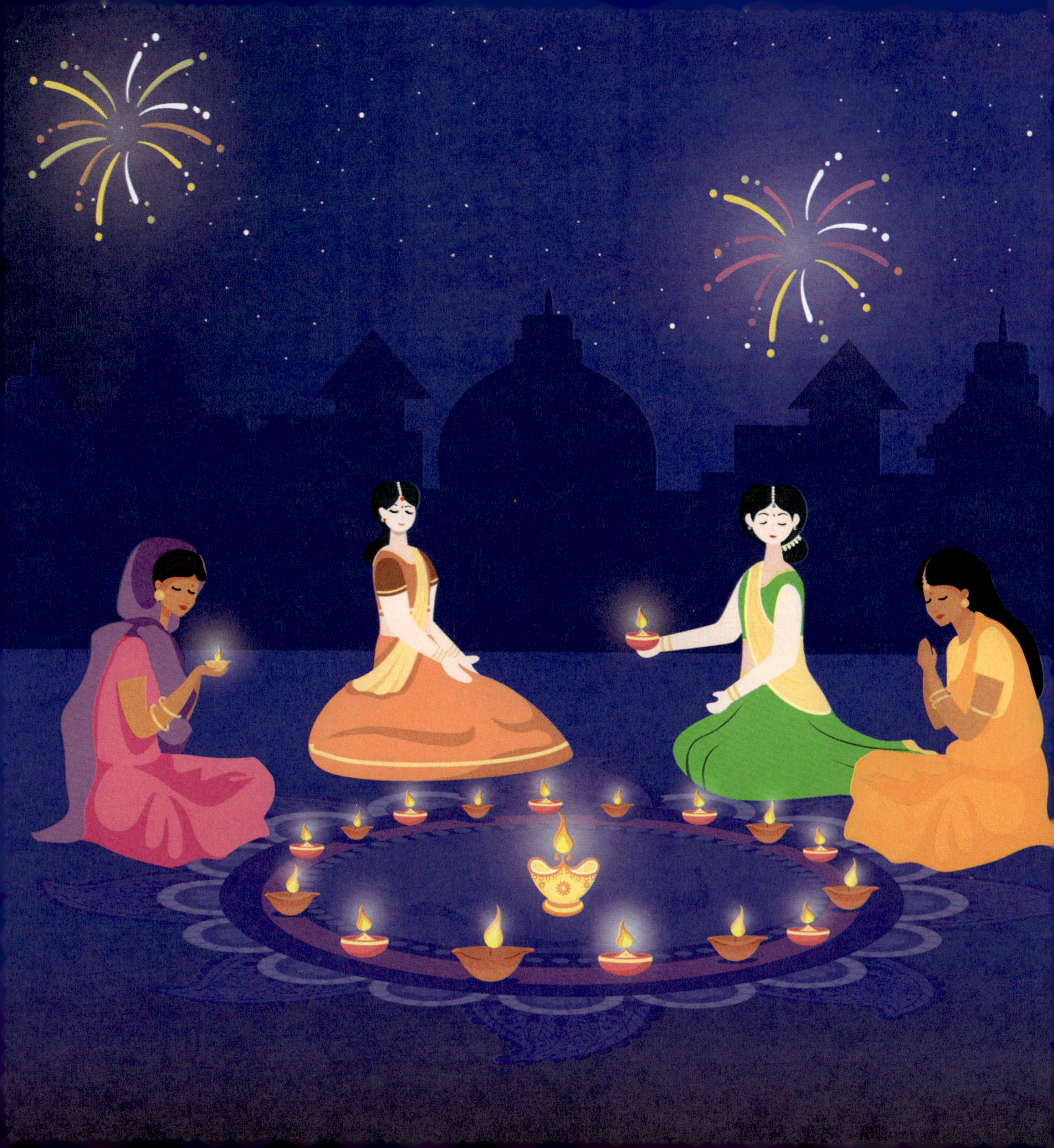

DAY 3
Lakshmi Puja

This is the most important day of Diwali celebrations, which falls on amavasya (the 30th day of the lunar month according to the Hindu calendar). During **Lakshmi Puja**, families gather for communal prayers to the goddess Lakshmi. Firecrackers and fireworks are let off in the evening.

Their purpose is to welcome the goddess and ward off dark powers.

DAY 4
Padua

The penultimate day of the festival is a time for family and friends. At that time, meals are eaten together and gifts are given.

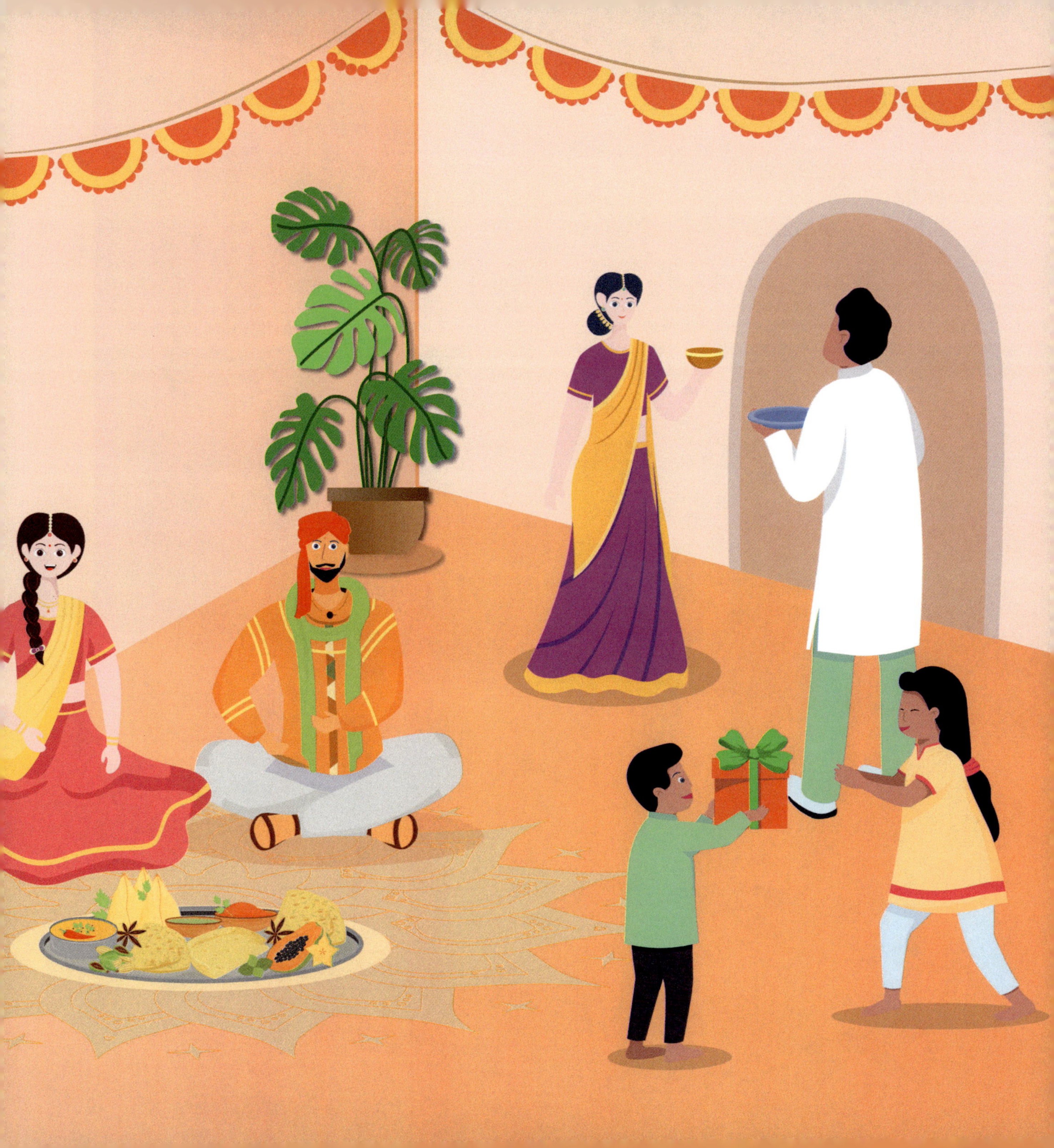

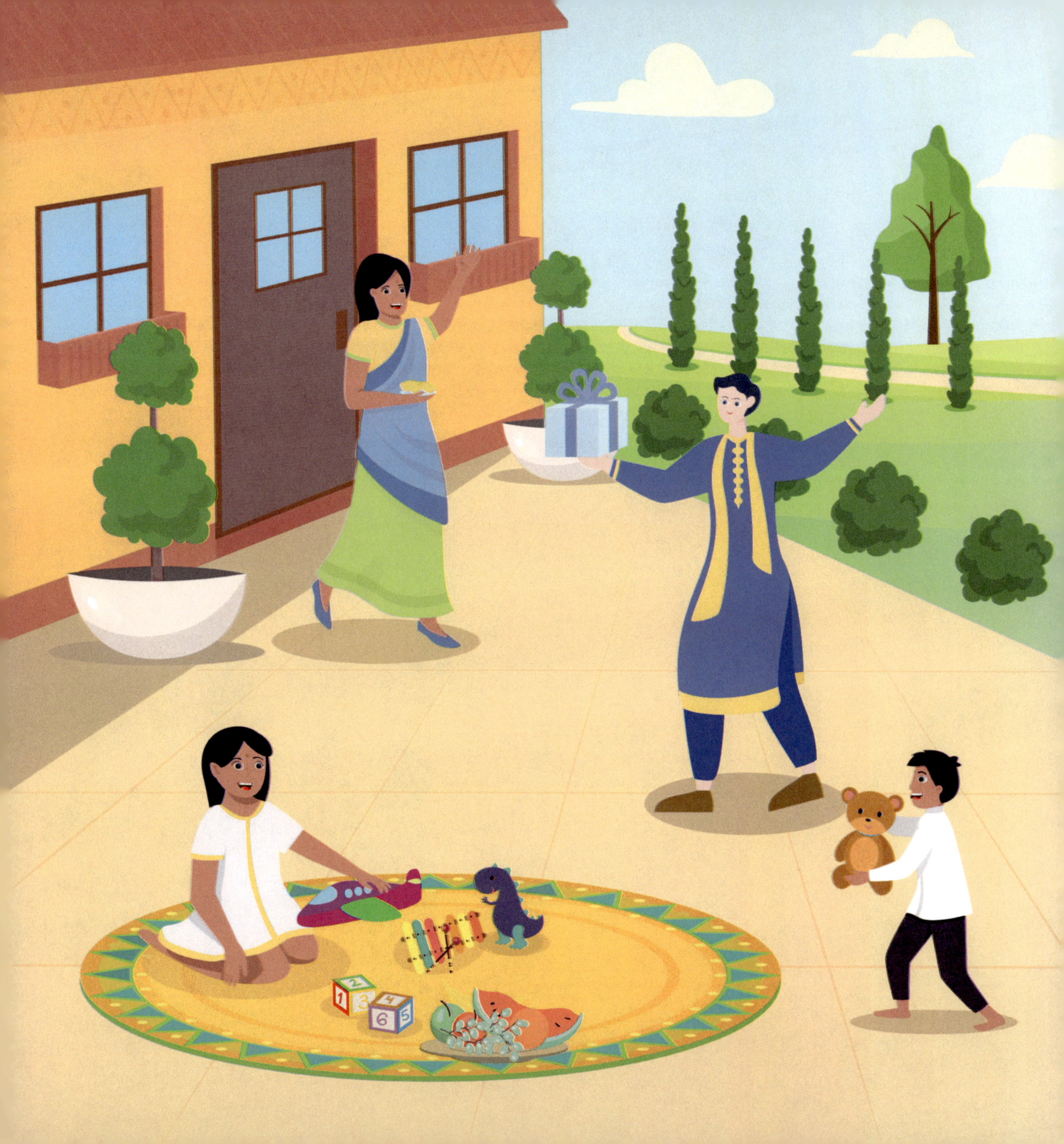

DAY 5
Bhai Duj

The last day of the celebration is a day of brotherly love. Brothers visit their married sisters.

They spend time together eating lunch and praying for happiness and prosperity for each other.

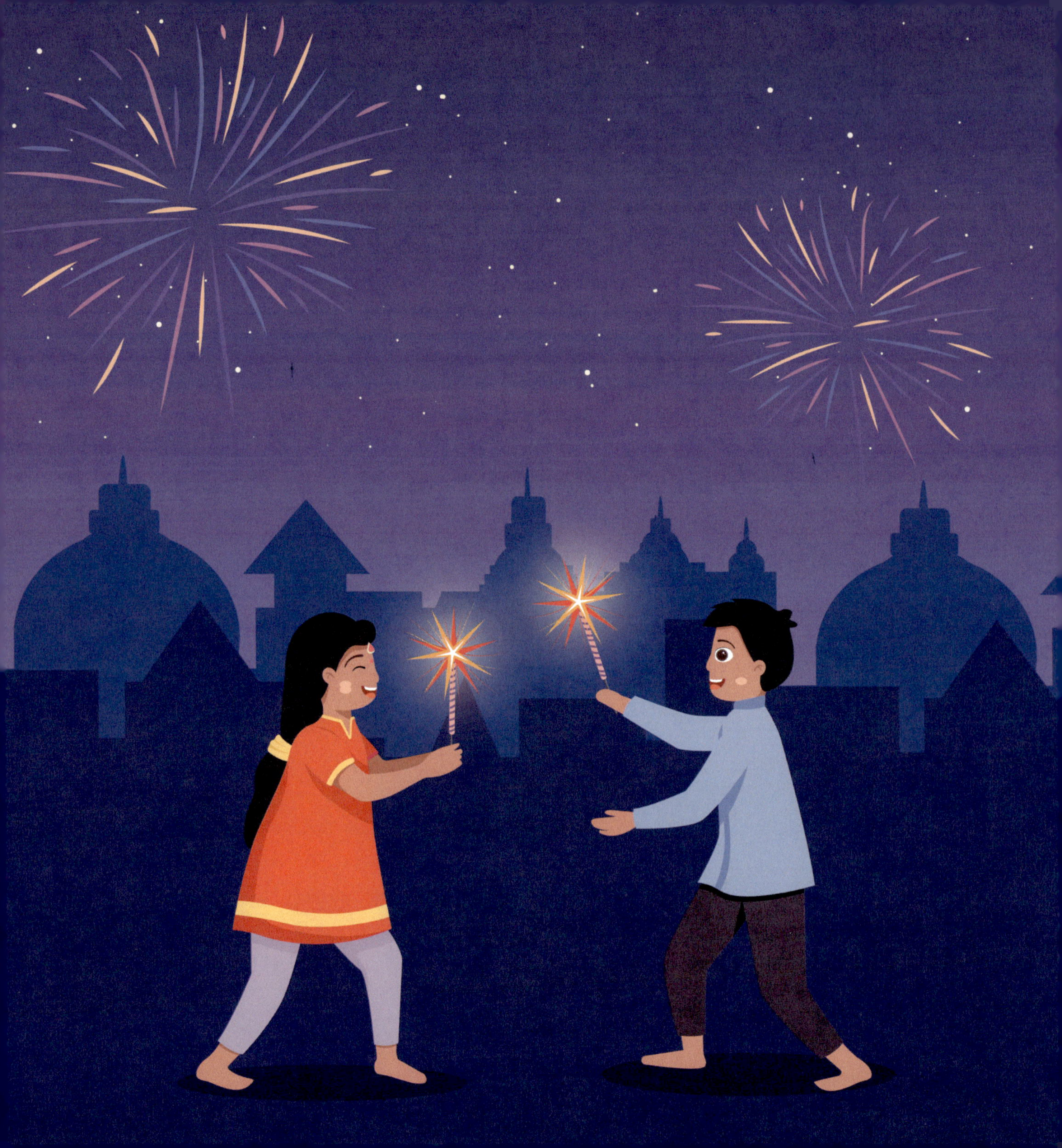

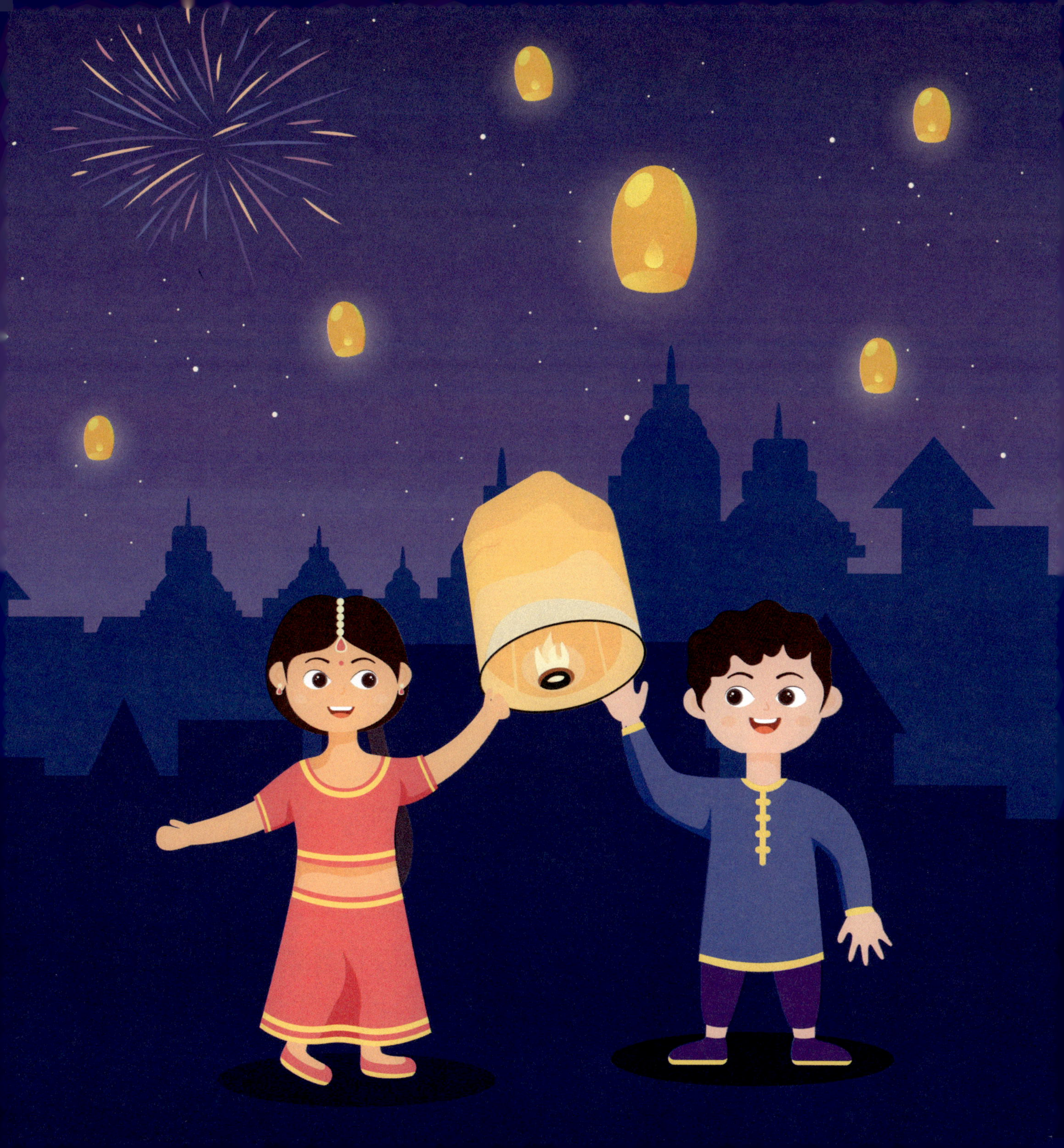

Feasting is part and parcel of the tradition of any joyous holiday. Indians also prepare their own traditional dishes to celebrate Diwali. Here are some of them:

Chakli

Crispy deep-fried rice flour snacks

Coconut Barfi

Dessert made of condensed milk and sugar with flaked coconut

Kaju barfi

A dish of milk and cashew nuts formed into the shape of a diamond

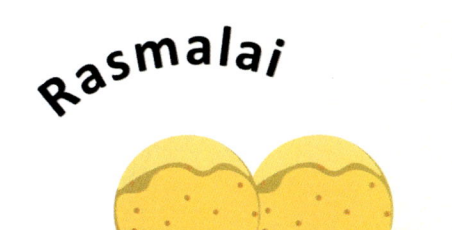

Rasmalai

Chhana curd cheese dessert, spiced with saffron and cardamom

Please leave a review - I'd love to know it!

The festival of lights in India is a very intense time for followers of Hinduism. Diwali is accompanied by joy and gratitude for family, friends and the victory of light over darkness.

Made in the USA
Las Vegas, NV
30 October 2023

79943681R10019